# Dad's Special Loving Daughters

(100 Poems)

by
Michael Lewis

Copyright © 2020 by Michael Lewis.

ISBN-978-1-6485-8116-8

All rights reserved. No part of this book may be reproduced or transmitted in any form or by any means, electronic or mechanical, including photocopying, recording, or by any information storage and retrieval system, without permission in writing from the copyright owner.

The views expressed in this work are solely those of the author and do not necessarily reflect the views of the publisher, and the publisher hereby disclaims any responsibility for them.

Matchstick Literary
1-888-306-8885
orders@matchliterary.com

## About the Author

Michael Lewis is dedicated to the happiness of his family. He is the Daddy of family of a six girls, who have been his loving treats for approximately 35 years. The girls include his wife Brenda, his four daughters Rollie, Leigh-Anne, Chelsea, and Sarah, and Sarah's spouse Melissa. During the family's lifetime, the six of them have received about one hundred and fifty poems each written by Daddy. They always enjoy his poems on special occasions every year and love each one they receive.

Michael, the Daddy, completed his college studies at the University of Tennessee where he received a Masters degree in Industrial Engineering. He spent his professional working career on engineering projects. He has added to his technical work a talented part-time writer on his own and received consistent high recognition from his girls for the poems written for them.

Michael used his professional leadership skills in his full-time job for large service and production companies. However, he consulted on the side of his career with part-time help for some twelve organizations like the Pal's Restaurant Services and the Holston Army Ammunition Plant. His support to them led them to implement Quality Management requirements. With Michael's help they won the National Quality Management Award presented to them by the U.S. President and Chief Army Officers.

During Michael's full lifetime he attended Methodist, Episcopal and Presbyterian churches with a strong Christiam belief and regular worship of God and Jesus Christ. Michael developed poems for his six girls covering their lifetime Christian beliefs. This book is written to as many people as possible for their importance and entertainment. Michael wants to give to every girl in the world what he has given to his own wonderful girls.

# Contents

1. Poems for Dad's Daughters (24) .................................................... 1

2. Birthdays for Dad's Daughters (15) ............................................... 31

3. Christmas for Dad's Young Daughters (9) ..................................... 49

4. Christmas for Dad's Teenage Daughters (9) ................................. 59

5. Christmas for Dad's Adult Daughters (10) .................................... 71

6. Valentines for Dad's Daughters (21) .............................................. 85

7. Easter for Dad's Daughters (7) .................................................... 107

8. Thanksgiving for Dad's Daughters (5) ........................................ 115

9. The Ending of Dad's Poems ....................................................... 121

# Preface

Hi! I'm Michael Lewis.

Up until 38 years ago, I was just a professional engineer for large chemical companies, restaurants, hospitals, and others who wanted me to help them improve their quality systems for national awards. I was consistently able to help all of them with three of them winning national quality awards.

Then I had my wife and first girl child who became more important than anything else in my life. Time continued over the next 7 years until I had 3 more daughters who became just as impressive and loveable as the first. One of my daughters grew up and married another wonderful female. With my wife one of the group, this brought me a family of 6 wonderful girls today.

Through their presence, I inherited dozens of great knowledge about how positive, entertaining and exciting the ideas that were brought to me by my girls. These ideas from observing them provided me great material for writing the girls poems on special occasions.

I have saved individual copies of poems I wrote for my wife and daughters. I wrote these mostly on Birthdays, Christmas, Valentines, Thanksgiving, Special Occasions, and more. I have saved copies of the poems I have written during these 35 years for my 6 special girls.

Up until now, I have saved copies of these poems privately because they were meant to be only for my individuals receiving them. However, I have thought recently that your girls should be given these copies and also for their fathers and mothers to enjoy. Someone in your group may be motivated to work parts of them into communications to another girl or boy. Whatever reason and motivation you have, I wish you a positive reason for having this book.

Good Luck to You!!

# The History Behind the Author (Dad) and his Book:

Dad's birth (Michael's) was to his Mom and Dad in the year 1951.

As a child he immediately started attending the neighborhood's Fairview United Methodist Church on a steady basis.

His parents provided positive encouragement and support for everything he did.

He was a small child around 2 years old when he became extremely close to wonderful neighbors such as Mrs. Chase and Mrs. Rogers.

During his childhood he loved a close relationship with his Grandfather Lewis and Grandmother Burton (two helpful and perfect Christians).

At 6 years old he entered the 1st Grade under a woman teacher he loved, Mrs. Williams.

Over the next grade classes and middle schools, he did extremely well and had many significant passed scores.

In Middle School, he had extremely good English grades from Mrs. Hartman.

In Middle School, he was educated well on National and Tennessee History by Mr. Herman Tester.

In High School, he was regionally recognized as its third best student for his Math capabilities provided by his teacher Mr. Gary Stafford.

In High School, he started on the basketball team for head coach, Mr. Hobart Powell.

In High School, he started on the baseball team for head coach, Mr. Herman Tester.

As a teenager, he had a number of friends having fun together (Bill, David, Sonny, Carl).

He had a number of teenage girl friends and cousins (especially sister Kathy).

He learned to not judge other people's attitude, mistakes and faults, but to admire their nationality, skin color, language, financial situation, Christianity, and treating you as a positive person.

He had some very talented math and engineering professors at the Univ. Tennessee.

He found and married a perfect, loving wife of Brenda.

They had four daughters born between 1981 and 1987.

He learned and enjoyed his work under Holston Defense Corporate presidents, John Bearden and Al King.

He had wonderful relationships with four Christian Ministers who built his Christian confidence: Doug Berndt Episcopal, Jack Raymore Presbyterian, Dan Clark Presbyterian, and Collin (and wife Blair) Adams Presbyterians.

He has had many adult friends (male and female) who continue to build his confidence and maturity in Christ Jesus.

He views his four daughters, now adults, who have motivated him over the past 35 years to write poems for them on a regular basis because they share his love.

For Dad, everything in his life (including writing the materials used in this book over the past 35 years) was made possible by his Trust and Faith in Christ Jesus.

I hope you get some closeness to Christ Jesus by reading these poems!

# 1

*Poems for Dad's Daughters (24)*

## *Slide Down A Rainbow*

Climb up a moon beam,
Swing on a star;
Slide down a rainbow,
Throw me kisses from afar.

Bounce on the clouds,
Fly high in the sky;
Slide down a rainbow,
Give me hugs as you go by.

Swim in the rainbow,
Shine bright like the sun;
Slide down a rainbow,
Always love me little one.

## *If Only I Could*

I wish I could erase all the miles,
That lay between here and there;
If I could I would so that nothing would ever
Keep me from having you near.

I wish I could command the sun,
To shine on you and me each day;
If I could I would hide the clutter,
That blocks our view and gets in the way.

I wish I could harness the wind
To always blow from you to me;
If I could I would do so I'd always know
Where to look so that only you I would see.

I wish I could make time stand still
Until once again with you I could be;
If I could I would so that I didn't miss
One moment of all your joy and glee.

I wish I could join our spirits
To always remain one and totally real;
If I could I would so that we could share
Every single thing we experience and feel.

I wish I could have only the good things
That make me feel warm, happy and free;
If I could I would choose to have you,
To spend every day of life with me.

# You're Part of Me, Girl

You're part of me Girl
Like two melons in a patch;
Like two cookies in a batch,
Like two itches wanting a scratch.

You're part of me Girl
Like two berries on a vine;
Like two cones on a pine,
Like two pimples on a behind.

You're part of me Girl
Like two bumps on a log;
Like two fleas on a dog,
Like two tits on a hog.

You're part of me Girl
Like two bees on a bun;
Like two coons on the run,
Like two monkeys having fun.

You're part of me Girl
Like two stars in the sky;
Like two wings on a fly,
Like two gas tanks that are dry.

You're part of me Girl
And I'm part of you;
Accept it because it's true,
There's nothing you can do.

## A Kitten's Bed Time

Time for bed my little kitten,
Time to end another day;
Say a prayer for all your blessings
In your sweet and innocent way.

Time for bed my little kitten,
Time to put up all your things;
Let me lay you on a warm cloud
And cover you up with Angel wings.

Time for bed my little kitten,
Time to lay you softly down;
So rest a minute upon my shoulder
While I sing a restful sound.

Time for bed my little kitten,
Time for starry, moonlit skies;
Listen to God's peaceful silence
And close those sparkling, soft blue eyes.

Time for bed my little kitten,
Time to tuck you snugly in;
Dream about our times together
And when you wake, we'll play again.

Time for bed my little kitten,
Time to soothe your tender heart;
May my love be always with you
And may we never, ever part.

## *Preparations*

You were conceived to be a darling princess,
You arrived on wings from the endless skies;
You were born amid lofty hopes and dreams,
You were special in everyone's eyes.

You were nurtured on the milk of angels
You were raised with adoration and love;
You were cuddled in the arms of glory,
You were rocked to sleep on soft clouds above.

You were bathed in the waters of purity,
You were clothed in the gowns of grace;
You were schooled in the halls of success,
You were granted a good conscience and pretty face.

You were given a head that knows its surroundings,
A heart that understands hurt and need;
You were given hands that offer a kind, tender touch,
And a soul of rejoicing that also knows how to bleed.

You were baptized with fire, water and spirit,
You learned how confidence and humility can abide;
You were taught the arts of forgiveness and mercy,
In your heart happiness and peace will always reside.

You were dealt a dose of fear and adversity,
And then were taught the right way to get through it;
You've been given the best that life has to give,
Now get Yourself out there and Just Do It.

## *If I Had a Ball*

If I had a ball, I'd bounce it a bunch,
All day at work on the floor with a crunch,
Right through my breaks and my lunch.

If I had a bat, I'd swing it all day,
With a swift swoosh and a sway
At everything that came my way.

If I played a game, I'd play it to win,
From the finish to the begin,
Over and over, again and again.

If I went to school, I*'d want to be the teacher's best,*
Ace every homework, quiz and test,
Make better grades than all the rest.

If I had a dog, I'd want to have more than one tail,
Either wings or a mast for a big sail,
And be able to fetch my slippers and the nail.

If I had a girl, I'd be stuck to her like glue,
She'd be sweet as honey dew,
Kind and beautiful just like you.

## My Special Little One

Dance in the street,
Sour through the air;
Leap like a frog,
Fly if you dare.

Let out a cheer,
Beam like the sun;
I think we should celebrate,
Cause you're a special little one.

# Great Day For UP

UP in the morning,
UP out of bed;
If you were a bunny,
You'd have pointy ears on your head.

UP to get ready,
UP to the fast pace;
If you were a puppy,
You'd have whiskers on you face.

UP to go to school,
UP to work, play and eat;
If you have a kitten,
You'd have claws on your feet.

UP to have practice and lessons,
UP to have telephone calls and mail;
If you were a skunk,
You'd have a stripe upon your tail.

UP to life and happiness,
Up to love and UP to you;
If you were anything but my girl
I wouldn't know what to do.

# Viewing You

Way down in a cavern,
High up in the sky;
Far off over yonder,
Close to eye-to-eye.

Dark and dim in a corner,
Bright and crisp on a lighted stage;
Cool and calm on an autumn morning,
Hot and fiery in a stormy rage.

Crystal clear through mountain water,
Obscure and fuzzy through a foggy haze;
Right up front and out in the open,
In the shadows on cloudy days.

No matter when and how I view you,
In plain, whole sight or only in part;
You shine bright like a blazing comet,
And put warmth in my cold, old heart.

# You for Me

When I see you smile,
It brings sunshine to my day;
When I hear you laugh,
I laugh back in a crazy way.

When I touch your hand,
All the barriers begin to fall;
When I know your thoughts,
I begin to understand it all.

When I kiss your cheek,
All your beauty is there to see;
When I feel you're close,
The world opens up for me,

When you're far away,
I don't know what to do;
When I stop and look,
There's nothing more special than you.

## Two Little Kittens

Two little kittens,
All furry and warm;
Two little kittens,
Safe from any harm.

Two little kittens,
All playful and sweet;
Two little kittens,
A wonderful treat.

Two little kittens,
Together to stay;
Two little kittens,
Always to play.

Two little kittens,
So happy and jolly;
Two little kittens,
My friends and Dolly.

Two little kittens,
Watch them grow and grow;
Two little kittens,
I love you both so.

## Wishes, Hopes and Dreams

Hopes and wishes are my reasons,
Dreams are the light for my way;
Prayers give me comfort during my journey,
Love keeps me going day after day.

My wishes outnumber the stars in the sky,
My dreams would fill-up a book;
My prayers cover the face of the earth,
Almost everything and everywhere you look.

If all of my prayers could be answered,
And all of my dreams could possibly come true;
If I could have everyone of my wishes,
I'd make sure that I would always have you.

# How Much Do I Love Thee?

How high is the moon?
How deep is the sea?
How big is a rainbow?
That's how much you mean to me.

How tall is a mountain?
How fresh is morning dew?
How bright is the sunshine?
That's how fond I am of you.

How solid is a rock?
How strong is a bear?
How mighty is an oak tree?
That's how much I love and care.

How soft is a baby?
How hot is a fire?
How wet is the rain?
You are my heart's desire.

How true is a fact?
How sure are the stars above?
How long is forever?
You fill my heart with love.

## Guess Who?

Guess who likes your kisses?
Guess who likes your smiles?
Guess who gets just one hug?
To see you would drive hundreds of miles.

Guess who thinks you're pretty?
Guess who thinks you're smart?
Guess who would kiss an old hoot owl?
I have a piece of your heart.

Guess who really loves you?
Guess who thinks you're a star?
Guess who is really thankful?
That you are the sweet way you are.

## Tickle Me Darling

Tickle me tender,
Tickle me pink;
Tickle me so hard,
That I can't think.

Tickle me funny,
Tickle me blue;
Tickle me purple,
And I'll always love you.

Tickle me crazy,
Tickle me red;
Tickle me until
I lose my silly head.

Tickle me slowly,
Tickle me fast;
Tickle me orange,
And we'll have us a blast.

Tickle me silly,
Tickle me green;
Tickle my bones
Until they're skinny and lean.

Tickle me often,
Tickle me brown;
Tickle me until
My eyes roll on the ground.

Tickle me hot,
Tickle me cold;
Tickle me full of
Crazy wrinkles and folds.

Tickle me quiet,
Tickle me loud;
For now and forever
You will tickle me proud.

## *You Can Do It With Your Graduation*

The door is open,
The road is paved;
The till is filled,
The entry fee saved.

The opportunities are many,
The obstacles are few;
Our hopes are all high,
For the very best for you.

We're all mighty proud,
Of the fine person you are;
We know whatever you do,
You're going to go far.

Just stick to the lessons,
You've learned here at home;
Then you'll know what to do,
Wherever you choose to room.

So go for it all,
You have nothing to lose;
You have all that it takes
To get whatever you chose.

And when you have doubts,
Or when fear's in the way;
Draw comfort from us and from God,
Forever in your heart we'll stay.

## Magic and Sunbeams in Graduation

What can I say to a Graduate
Who had accomplished so many fine things?
What can I say to a Graduate
Who soars above as if she had eagle wings?

What can I say to a Graduate
Who shines brightly wherever she goes?
What can I say to a Graduate
Who evokes a smile from everyone she knows?

What can I say to a Graduate
Who impresses everyone she meets?
What can I say to a Graduate
Who makes a friend of everyone she greets?

What can I say to a Graduate
Who spreads goodwill all along her way?
What can I say to a Graduate
Who brings me joy and happiness every day?

What can I say to a Graduate
When she's the daughter of my dreams?
I say, "I love you, Proud of you,
Believe in you, Praying for you,
Behind you, I'll always find you,
I wish you a life of Magic and Sunbeams."

## Tough Questions

"What is the meaning of life?"
I asked the smart-looking bluebird;
She looked away toward the coming day
And flew off without a word.

"How important is fortune and fame?"
I inquired of the big horny toad;
He just ate one more bug, gave a little shrug
And hopped back across the road.

"Is money the most important thing of all?"
I queried the groundhog standing in the sun;
He met my eye and without even a goodbye
Into his hole he retreated on the run.

"Who really knows right things from wrong?"
I interrupted the meal of the fat wooly worm;
He took one last chew looking like he hadn't a clue
And crawled off with not the least little squirm.

"Where and why did it all begin?"
Was my question to the wise old owl;
He winked and he blinked while trying to think
Before clenching his jaws as if ready to growl.

"What is the Big Picture and Plan?"
I put to the lazy and muddy old pig:
He rolled and splashed and across the pen dashed
Before swallowing a fat knotty hickory twig.

"What could it all possibly mean?"
I said to the smelly and stubborn old mule;
He pawed and stomped and rowdily romped
Then chewed on some briars with a big slobbery drool.

"What made it all worthwhile?"
I offered to a turtle looking all sassy and jolly;
She answered, "Hippity-hop, Bibbity-bop,
Tomatoes, Lettuce, Cantaloupes, and My Dolly."

# A Happy Father's Prayer (No. 1)

I asked for a girl
And the Lord gave me four;
I asked for a challenge,
And He moved one in the door.

I asked for some space
And the Lord pointed me to the sky;
I asked for excitement,
And He said, "Go ahead and try to fly."

I asked for some friends
And He gave me a constant ringing phone;
I asked for lots of money,
And He showed me where I could get a big loan.

I asked for good looks,
And the Lord gave me eyes;
I asked for success,
And He gave me many Hell-of-a-Good-Deal buys.

I asked for happiness,
And He gave me a new frisky, barking dog;
I asked for contentment,
And He made me look and sleep like a log.

I asked for love,
And the Lord gave me you;
I asked the Lord for many blessings,
And He gave me more than I know what to do.

# A Happy Father's Prayer (No. 2)

Some Angels have wings,
And magical things,
And songs that only an Angel sings.

Some Angels fly high,
Above the heavenly sky,
And laugh and play and never cry.

Some Angels wear gowns,
And have solid gold crowns,
And never get hurt by falling down.

Some Angels are white,
And sparkle like starlight,
And visit little girls in their dreams at night.

But My Angel is You,
With pretty eyes of blue,
You're more special than any Christmas Angel, too.

Some Angels have wings,
And magical things,
And songs that only an Angel sings.

Some Angels fly high,
Above the heavenly sky,
And laugh and play and never cry.

Some Angels wear gowns,
And have solid gold crowns,
And never get hurt by falling down.

Some Angels are white,
And sparkle like starlight,
And visit little girls in their dreams at night.

## *Daydreams and Goals*

When I was just a little boy,
I daydreamed almost everywhere;
I imagined places I wanted to go,
And of what I'd be when I got there.

I dreamed while sitting on the bed,
While in the bath, and even in school;
I fantasized to feel satisfied,
And to stay healthy, warm and cool

I escaped in thought to keep from getting bored,
From getting lonely and even from getting lost;
I dreamed of winning at sports and games,
And of being the hero that everyone admired most.

But my favorite daydreams were of Pride and Joy,
Of Peace and Hope and Love;
Of having a beautiful daughter just like you
That forever I would Cherish and Be Most Proud Of.

# Life Can Be So Boring

Life can be so boring,
New kicks are much too few;
It seems the same old things
Are all that we ever do.

It's school, practice and lessons,
Lots of other work to do;
New books, new food,
New movies are much too few.

Life can be so boring,
New kicks are much too few;
Same house, same car, same bed,
Same old chores to do.

Same hat, same coat, same gloves,
Same old socks, same old shoe;
Samme sun, same moon, same stars,
Same wind, rain and dew.

Same face, nails and hair,
Same body with which to do;
Same ears, eyes, hands, and feet,
All in the same old pairs of two.

Life can be so boring,
New kicks are much too few;
But all these same old boring things,
Are making a Fine Young Lady of you.

# Look Straight Ahead, Daddy

Look Straight Ahead, Daddy
Not up in the sky;
You might trip over a hound dog,
As you go walking by.

Look Straight Ahead, Daddy
Not down at the ground;
You might miss all the fireworks,
Right here and all around.

Look Straight Ahead, Daddy
Not off to the side;
You might run into a Daffy Donkey,
Who will take you for a ride.

Look Straight Ahead, Daddy
Not over at another;
If I have to say it again,
I'm going to tell your Mother.

Look Straight Ahead, Daddy
Just look straight at me;
I'm the most special thing
That you will ever see.

## I'm Going to Get You Real Good

I'm going to get you real good,
If you don't give me a big smile;
I'll paint your face all brown and black,
And take you to church for a while.

I'm going to get you real good,
If you don't mind exactly what I say;
I'll hand you up by your littlest toes
And leave you there for your nap on Saturday.

I'm going to get you real good,
If you don't give me a kiss right now;
I'll fill your bed with pigs and goats,
And make you sleep with an old dirty cow.

I'm going to get you real good,
If you don't give me just what I ask;
I'll gather up all of your baby dolls,
And glue on them an ugly Halloween mask.

I'm going to get you real good,
If you don't talk to me on the phone;
I'll give your puppy green beans to eat,
And give you a nasty old dog bone.

I'm going to get you real good,
If you don't love me forever, ever more;
I've put you in a barrel of rotten apples,
Until you are rotten to the core.

I'm going to get you real good,
Just you wait and see;
The next time I see you, I'll snatch you right up,
And take you home with me.

## *Do You Know?*

Do you know how much I've missed you,
How many different ways I've cared?
Do you know how many times I've kissed you,
How many special moments we've shared?

Do you know how many boys all the girls have dumped,
How many tender hearts you will break?
Do you know how many times the average cricket jumped,
How many baths the average bird takes?

Do you know how many miles Christopher Columbus sailed,
How many B's, C's, D's, and F's are made?
Do you know how much time all the losers have killed,
How much sunshine there is and how much shade?

Do you know how many thoughts go through my head,
How many people have seen pro baseball teams play?
Do you know how many nails are polished bright red,
How many lips are painted each day?

Do you know how much water has gone under the bridge,
How much God's work is left to do?
Do you know how much of this earth is on a ridge,
Do you know How Much I Love You?

# 2

*Birthdays for Dad's Daughters (15)*

# My Girl's Happy Birthday

Give her some happiness,
More than anything else to give;
Bring in her family and friends,
To help her feel great to live.

Give her a party,
For making cheers and joy;
Give her balloons and whistles,
To bring joy to every girl and boy.

Give her a calendar,
To figure how young there is to know;
Give her some knowledge,
To know how far her life should grow.

Give me the Lord Jesus,
To completely watch herself all around;
Give her Daddy's heart to her,
Who loves her well beyond bound.

# What Is It?

What is rounder than a grapefruit,
And bigger than a peach?
What is lighter than a big bouncy ball
That you play with on the beach?

What is lighter than a pancake,
And higher than a cloud?
What is brighter than a peacock
Strutting around tall and proud?

What is softer than a pillow,
And sweeter than a plum?
What is crisper than a carrot,
And the beat of a drum?

What is prettier than a butterfly,
And nicer than a baby to hold?
No, silly dilly not a hot air balloon,
But my special daughter at 4 years old.

## Ready for Your Birthday?

What is lighter than a feather,
And brighter than a sunshine ray?
What has more color than a rainbow,
And prettier than new flowers on a Springtime day?

What is smoother than a silky gown,
And softer than a baby's cheeks?
What is happier than a party bug,
And more fun than a new puppy that squeaks?

What is sweeter than a honey bee,
And nicer than a little flutter?
What is fancier than a painted wing,
And richer than real cream and butter?

What is more special than a birthday,
And warmer than a kitten to hold?
No, Silly Dilly, not a butterfly,
But my special daughter is 8 years old.,

## Wishes for You

I wish I might,
I wish I may;
Wish a happy wish for you,
On your Sixth birthday.

I wish you Six candles,
On a Six-layer cake;
I wish you Six wishes,
That you decide to make.

I wish you Six rainbows,
I wish you a bright sun;
I wish you Six party games,
And Six loads of birthday fun.

I wish you Six surprises,
Sixty laughs, and Six hundred smiles;
I wish you Six thousand friends,
To visit and play for a while.

I wish you the very best,
I wish you the most;
I wish you all good things,
From the mountain, desert and coast!

I wish I might,
I wish I may;
Wish a happy wish for you,
On your SIXTH Birthday.

# What Do You Say?

What do you say to a cupcake,
With icing of pretty pink and blue?
What do you say to a new red rose,
That is moist with the fallen dew?

What do you say to the ocean,
Reflecting the full moon's light?
What do you say to a candle,
As it shines brightly in the night?

What do you say to an angel,
That has touched you from above,
What do you say to a pretty face,
Who smiles that sweet smile of love?

What do you say to a kiss,
That is given from a 9-year old heart?
What do you say to a daughter,
Who's been just perfect from the start?

## Sparkling Eyes

Grab a handful of balloons,
Spread Your wings like a bird;
Beat on a big loud drum,
Because "Happy" is your birthday word.

Toot on a brass horn,
Make happy tunes fill the sky;
Blow out all Seven candles,
And smile with a sparkling wish in your eye!

# A Blessed Life for You

Every morning I awake at home,
Here in my favorite place to be;
I first think of how mice you always are,
And how beautiful you are to see.

All of my days are really nice,
As you grow more as an adult all the way;
You apply very wise decision making,
Reminding you to do right things every day.

I'm reminded that this is your special birthday,
The many first years filling you with the best;
Your life makes me happy for having you,
Obtaining your cure, your love and more of the rest.

You standard blessing days are important,
And you are a wonderful person for me;
Blessings are important for you to maintain,
Like one of many Angels in Heaven to be.

You and I have special blessings for everything,
Our wonderful Father God is always here;
Jesus is here every day with more blessings for us,
Providing lots of Love to help make you dear.

# *The Reason for Your Great Birthday*

My Daughter? My Daughter?
Who in the world is you?
Are you my special Daughter?
Are there special things you do?

Do you talk to me often?
Do you say special things to me?
Do you focus on things to get my attention?
Do you know your special things for me to see?

Do you look to see what's in my heart?
Do you look to see what's in my eye?
Do you look inside of me often?
Do you know just how much I try?

Do you know how much you are close to me?
Do you know how much I care?
Do you see it all inside of me for you?
Do you know how much Love for you I wear?

Do you know I celebrate your Birthdays?
Do you know my Love for you is in place?
Do you know for you my life is full of happiness?
Do you know that Jesus shares for me His grace?

## *Perfection of Your Birthday*

There was a perfect girl,
Who lived a perfect life;
She was destined to find a perfect husband,
And to become a perfect wife.

She had a perfect car,
And drove it many perfect miles;
She had a perfectly pretty face,
That smiled many perfectly pretty smiles.

She lived in a perfect State,
The Greenest in the perfect land of the free;
She graduated from a perfect University,
The Orangest, most perfect school you ever did see.

She was accepted for a perfect internship,
In a perfect Big City Place;
There were perfect people running everywhere,
All going at perfect Break-neck pace.

She moved into a perfect apartment,
And filled it with perfect furniture perfectly new;
She had all the perfect conveniences,
Including a perfect washer and perfect dryer, too.

She had a pretty Mom,
And a truly perfect Dad;
Together they were the most perfect parents,
That a Perfect Girl ever had.

## *Hello and Goodbye Sweetheart*

It is exciting and it is scary,
It is full of hopes as well as fears;
It is the beginning and the ending,
It is the little moments more than the years.

It has some gains and some losses,
It has some old and some new;
It has the past and the present,
But mostly it's about the future of you.

It has had its pain and its pleasures,
We've been lost and found at times along the way;
This is both Hello and Goodbye Sweetheart,
You've passed from Childhood to Womanhood Today!

## *Another Year, Another Birthday*

Another year, another Birthday,
Thank goodness for God giving You His way.

You have so many good habits to keep,
Always making me receive them so deep.

You always make me feel so strong,
Times with You are never being so long.

You have a lot of good things to bring,
Your things are so nice they make my heart sing.

I would never live in this world without you,
So much I would have trouble in all that I do.

Thank You for being such a great Daughter of Love,
Keep your Birthday Happy and real with God above!

# *Maybe The Best Birthday of All*

It's Birthday time again for you,
There are special things that you will find to do.

It's because you are wonderful and kind,
You have a warm heart and joyful mind.

I always feel extra lucky with you all the time,
You have what it takes to be so fine.

I think about you in depth everyday,
Making me feel like yours in my own happy way.

Father God and Jesus Christ as always new,
They have given me someone as great as you.

## I Just Don't Know

I just don't know what you are doing,
Where you are, where you want to go;
I don't know how many friends you have,
Or how distant to those you choose not to know.

I don't know how many jokes and stories you tell,
Whether you're laughing or crying all the time;
I don't know how happy or sad you are,
If you feel being awake not asleep is a crime.

I don't know what's on you mind,
Whether you try to or not at all to think;
I don't know what you make sure you eat,
And how often you have a drink.

I can't talk to you so I don't know much,
I try to find your secret or make a guess;
I can't tell how much you know about your sisters,
If you wear blouses and pants or a skirt or dress.

I don't know how much weight you've lost,
Or instead you are having a weight gain;
I don't know if you're rich or poor,
How good you feel, how much you suffer in pain.

I don't know what your age is,
But I know what year you were born;
I don't know whether you're a full adult yet,
I think your Birthday starts with the 21st Morn.

I don't know how hard you work,
How much free time you have and where you go;
I hope you know how much I Love You,
Just tell me about yourself sometime and I will know.

## *Older and Free*

Older and free, whatever you want,
Whatever you want to be;
Whenever and wherever you want to go,
You can try to have and do and see.

You are young and can act young,
You can dream and make it come true;
You can fly, you can swim, you can jump,
Anything you want to do.

You can like and love whatever,
And whoever that you choose;
You can try and risk whatever,
And not worry if you lose.

You can think it and say it,
You can accept and experience and feel;
You can live without dread, worry or fear,
You can search for what's true and real.

You can be optimistic and positive,
Happy and healthy as can be;
You can be entertained and full of life,
That's definitely your Birthday and free.

## Another Day, Another Gift

It's another day in your life,
Another special time to rejoice;
A time for you to be your usual beauty,
A time to use your wonderful voice.

You can smile with as much as you want,
It's a great way for you to easily be;
You can laugh at nice things at hand,
Many things of real joy to have and see.

You can share happiness with all around you,
Accepting their gifts for your Birthday too;
You can share your happiness with those you care for,
Giving back love with the ones who have it for you.

All those things are great in your regard,
Enjoying your life as you do so good;
But even better is me and Jeus sharing your heart,
You are as special to us as you possibly could.

# 3

*Christmas for Dad's Young Daughters (9)*

# *The True Spirit of Christmas*

She awakened one day from a short winter's nap,
She was just old enough to climb up into my lap;
She wanted to hear stories about the Jolly Old Man,
I said, "I'll tell you what I know, as much as I can."

I told her he's friendly, he's happy, he's not to be feared,
I described his big rosy cheeks and his long snowy white beard;
I explained how he granted wishes and makes dreams come true,
I warned, "You'd better be good, so he'll be good to you."

I told her how important it was for her to believe,
How he says it's much better to give than it is to receive;
How many souls in this world are not as well off as us,
How Santa makes no distinction over whom he makes a fuss.

I look in her eyes as they sparkle with an innocent glow,
I hugged and kissed her until my heart began to overflow;
It was one of many times that my little girl gave warmth and joy to me,
And I felt The True Spirit of Christmas sitting there on my knee.

# Let's Go Down to Bethlehem

Let's go down to Bethlehem,
And find the manger bed;
Where Mary and Joseph stopped to rest,
Where Baby Jesus lays his head.

Let's go down to Bethlehem,
And see the golden star;
That brought the kings and wisemen
With gifts from lands afar.

Let's go down to Bethlehem,
And talk to the angels there;
Let's listen to their songs of joy,
And touch their wings and hair.

Let's go down to Bethlehem,
And hold the New-born King;
You can change His swaddling clothes,
And maybe I can sing.

Let's go down to Bethlehem,
And spend all Christmas Day;
If Baby Jesus likes you like I do,
He's sure to want to play.

# My Angel

Some Angels have wings,
And magical things,
And songs that only an Angel sings.

Some Angels fly high,
Above the heavenly sky,
And laugh and play and never cry.

Some Angels wear gowns,
And have solid gold crowns,
And never get hurt by falling down.

Some Angels are white,
And sparkle like starlight,
And visit little girls in their dreams at night.

But My Angel is You,
With pretty eyes of blue,
You're more special than any Christmas Angel, too.

## *Merry Christmas Heart*

Draw a Merry Christmas heart,
Make it special and neat;
Fill it up with Gummy Bears,
So it is sure to be sweet.

Draw a Merry Christmas heart,
Color it pretty and red;
Stuff it with fluffy snow,
And feed it on ginger bread.

Draw a Merry Christmas heart,
Kiss it until it's warm;
Don't let anyone break it,
Or try to bring it any harm.

Draw a Merry Christmas heart,
Love it until it's real;
Tell it all about us,
And the joy and love feel.

Draw a Merry Christmas heart,
Hug it like a tender heart bear;
Put it under our Christmas Tree,
To let Santa know that we care.

# Santa's Big Knee

Let me go to the mall,
And sit on Santa's big knee;
Let me sing, laugh and play,
And take His Jolly hug with me.

Let me tell him what I like,
And what toys He should bring me;
Let me get my picture made with Him,
So His beard will hang to see.

Let me tell Him I'm so sweet,
And I've been as good as I can be;
Let me kiss Him once, kiss Him twice,
So He won't dare forget me.

## My Little Angel Girl

Little Angel with soft golden hair,
Little Angel flying high in the air;
Little Angel sent from Santa Claus land,
Little Angel with marker marks on your hand.

Little Angel in your PJs and shoes,
Little Angel what Christmas gift do you choose?
Little Angel with a boo-boo on your knee,
Little Angel I choose you just for me.

## Santa's Gifts

Wrap Santa a Merry Christmas gift,
Make it all special and neat;
Put in a few gum drop bears,
So it is sure to be sugar sweet.

Wrap Santa a Merry Christmas gift,
With paper of green and red;
Add a handful of soft fluffy snow,
And some cookies of fresh ginger bread.

Wrap Santa a Merry Christmas gift,
One He is sure to be behold;
Throw in a kiss so soft and warm,
To help Him forget the harsh cold.

Wrap Santa a Merry Christmas gift,
Fill it up with sun beams and light;
Then top it off with a friendly smile,
That will last Him through the long night.

Wrap Santa a Merry Christmas gift,
Hug it tight like a loving old bear;
Put it all under your Christmas tree,
To let Santa know that you care.

# Christmas Gifts

I met a new group of balloons,
That I'd never seen before;
We all became light-headed friends,
And each one I truly adore.

There is Fred who is as red,
As Rudolph's shiny nose;
There's Julius who is orange,
And wears peelings instead of clothes.

There is Mellow who is yellow,
And smiles brightly all the time;
There is Jean who is green,
And is as flavorful as a lime.

There is Stu who is blue,
And sings every minute of every hour;
There is Violet who is purple,
And smells like a fragrant flower.

Then there's Daddy brown and round,
Who makes this group one less than seven;
And you who is sweet and pink,
And is an angel sent from heaven.

## *Christmas Star*

Christmas Star, Christmas Star,
Shining each and every night;
Just outside my window,
So true and joyfully bright.

Christmas Star, Christmas Star,
A candle will show the way;
A light of warmth and hope and love,
Bringing peace at the end of the day.

Christmas Star, Christmas Star,
A diamond with big brown eyes;
A face that glows like sunshine,
Through clear and cloudless skies.

Christmas Star, Christmas Star,
I watch with merry pride;
Admiring your radiant beauty,
And the sparkle you have inside.

Christmas Star, Christmas Star,
I close my eyes and pray;
And wish the wish that Daddys wish,
For their star on Christmas Day.

Christmas Star, Christmas, Star,
Twinking to let me know;
That her star light is shining so brightly,
As my daughter continues to grow.

# 4

*Christmas for Dad's Teenage Daughters (9)*

## Christmas To Me

You can hang all the lights and wreaths,
Then put up and trim the tree;
You can put the stockings by the fire,
And fill one to the top for me.

You can bake a truckload of cookies,
And make my favorite fudge if you dare;
You can wrap up a thousand presents,
And place pretty red bows on them with care.

You can string up a mistletoe ball,
And kiss me under it til I'm blue;
You can sing Rudolph and Silent Night,
And bring in Baby Jesus and our Santa, too.

You can light-up all the candles,
And line the street with luminaries there;
But it just won't seem like Christmas to me,
Not until my daughter has gotten here.

# Home For the Holidays

What was that noise I heard
Coming from the uppootsteps
It must have been something real,
Because I'm sure I heard it once before.

There goes that sound once again,
Like water running in the shower;
And I think I've been hearing footsteps
For a least a solid hour.

I wonder if my ears are playing tricks,
Creating nothing noises just to deceive me;
Those sounds are all so familiar,
But it's probably not what I hope it to be.

Now listen to that familiar sound,
It's a hair dryer don't you know;
And now music is coming from up there,
Like I used to hear a long time ago.

Someone must be coming down the stairs
With a cell phone ringing along the way;
Oh, thank you Lord, it's just what I'd hoped,
My daughter has come home for Christmas holiday.

## *My Christmas Wreath*

Whenever I see a Christmas wreath,
Decorated with pretty balls, ribbons and bows;
I'm reminded of my life circle that you complete,
And the pride and joy in you that I know.

 And if I could hang the perfect wreath this year,
I'd hang you on my heart to safely stay;
Making sure my circle remains unbroken,
And letting your confidence, care and love guide my way.

# *My Christmas Bell*

Whenever I hear a Christmas bell,
All silvery bright and ringing clear;
I think about your warm rings of joy,
And the sounds of love that you make here.

In many ways I was deaf from some special things,
Until God blessed me with a new heart and ears;
He gave me you and opened me up,
To a ringing love which I'll cherish for the rest of my years.

## *My Christmas Tree*

Whenever I decorate a Christmas tree
With ornaments of various beauty and kind;
The many talents you have and blessings you bring
Immediately come to my thankful heart and mind.

And if I could have the perfect tree this year,
I would top it off with just you alone;
Perched above the angels, bells and canes,
Spreading your warm kindness throughout my home.

# *My Christmas Luminary*

Whenever I see Christmas luminaries,
Bringing light to a normally darkened place;
I think of your great courage and spirit,
And the excitement that shines in your face.

Every heart has some dark spots where no light has been,
And mine too has some spots unvisited, unchallenged, and cold;
But by watching the brave way you tackle each situation and day,
A new light in me has made my heart a little more bold.

## My Obsessive, Compulsive Christmas

It was a cold, lonely Christmas,
And I was doing what seemed right;
I was flossing, brushing, gargling,
And shaving my whiskers most of the night.

It had been a long, hot shower,
And washed every cranny and nook;
I had scrubbed both of my ears
According to The Good Hygiene book.

Then out of the South,
I heard the great sound of jingling;
I was drawn in its direction,
The noise had set my heart a tingling.

And when I had found it,
It was my Daughter with her bells;
I asked, "What are you doing?"
"Bringing you Joy," she did tell.

I returned to my duties,
With Great Joy in my heart;
And I was lost for a moment,
Before I remembered where to restart.

I plucked some hairs from my nose,
And put some lotion on my feet;
I pulled my pants over my shoes,
And tucked my shirt in right neat.

Then from out of the North,
I felt a slight sense of calm notion;
And I was drawn nearer to it,
With a compelling swift motion.

And when I had reached it,
It was My Daughter with arms open wide;
I asked, "What are you doing?"
She said, "Bringing Peace to your side."

# Christmas Hug

I woke up this morning under my bed
Dreaming a dream just about you;
You were giving away hugs as Christmas gifts,
While I and hundreds more stood in line for a few.

I don't remember how we all got under my bed
Or who else you were giving hugs to;
But I remember the Happiness that we all felt,
And I just knew that God was hugging us through you.

So this year for you, my Daughter so sweet,
My Christmas Wish is a simple one I must say:
I only wish that God continues to give hugs through you,
In your lovely and loving way.

# Christmas for You and Me

You are my sweet little daughter,
I want you to stay close to me;
You put your best things around,
Best things you can have that I can see.

I don't see you as much as I used to,
The good things I want to go;
To know to see the best little times,
The little things I'm so lucky to know.

You're always saying nice things,
Seeing the best of me you can say;
Letting me know how nice you are,
The sweet comments you make me pay.

So how lucky we all really are,
Looking for outputting to be with you;
It's Jesus who knows you better than me,
He knew better in white and blue.

# 5

## Christmas for Dad's Adult Daughters (10)

## *There's Something Special About Christmas*

There's something special about Christmas
That sets my weary heart aglow;
There's something special about Christmas
That makes me want to be with the special people I know.

There's something special about Christmas
That makes me stop to consider those in need;
There's something special about Christmas
That makes me put aside my own selfish greed.

There's something special about Christmas
That makes me want to stop all of the world's pain;
There's something special about Christmas
That makes no act of kindness seem done in vain.

There's something special about Christmas
That makes me appreciate all that's mine;
There's something special about Christmas
That makes even the simplest gifts seem fine.

There's something special about Christmas
That makes a sad day bright;
There's something special about Christmas
That fills a dark world with light.

There's something special about Christmas
That points us in the right way;
There's something special about Christmas
That makes what's really important as clear as day.

There's something special about Christmas
That makes me want to give you a surprise;
There's something special about Christmas
That puts bright stars in the skies.

There's something special about Christmas
That makes me want to eat far too much;
There's something special about Christmas
That me close enough to Him to touch.

There's something special about Christmas
That makes me do things I don't normally do;
There's something special about Christmas
That makes me want even more to be with you.

# This Year's Christmas List

I made out a Christmas list for Santa
And this is what it said;
A new leather jacket, a sweater,
And a warm bogger for my head.

A book on the livers of Presidents,
A shovel for my yard;
One of those fancy, new wrenches,
That makes removing nuts not so hard.

A new golf club that will help me drive straight,
And make it easier to hit the ball;
A box of chocolates, a jar of strawberry jam,
And that's not nearly all.

I'd like my car detailed,
Or better yet I'd like a car that's all new;
But most of all I'd like a daughter
Who is as special and wonderful as you.

# You and Jesus Christ

The birth of Jesus reminds me of you,
He helps setup positive things for you to do;
He laid in a small manger of warm, soft hay,
Not the same place where you got to lay.

Your birth included a host of angels that first day,
Their important of you with Jesus led me to pray;
The Lord and you are helping me live with no fear,
Providing me with hope and comfort for my remaining years.

There were stars shining in the sky on your glorious birth day,
Stars for His birth and yours were bright in a maximum way;
Jesus and you are always giving me lots of natural pride,
Helping me have lots of success with each challenge at my side.

Jesus and you lead me to experience comforting dreams at night,
Every day of having Him and you near leads me to being right;
Having Him and you make me feel calm, tender and mild,
Able to live in heavenly peace with no current thoughts wild.

All that takes place for me since the beginning of you,
You give lots of wonderful happiness and joy to pursue;
I have the priority of praising Him and you for me,
I'll be loving Jesus and you during all my time to be.

# What Child is This

You were an extra special child,
With love first coming from Mom and Dad:
As a child you loved us both,
Being almost all the love we've had.

But you have received more from Jesus,
Who gives you more than we can give;
His is more than is available here on earth,
You have more love for Christ Jesus and us to live.

# *Silent Night*

Silent Night, Holy Night,
All is calm, nothing for you is fright;
You are here, you are known,
You are well loved by our family bright.

But Jesus loves you the most,
He's not silent about His light;
Jesus holds you above all else,
And your beauty is above our sight.

## *Silent Christmas Night*

It was during a Silent Night,
With not a sound to be heard;
He was suddenly among us,
And He offered a simple Word.

To you He said, "Go forth to every corner
Taking my purpose along the way;
Tell my story like only you can tell,
I'm depending on you today."

## Our Christmas for Christ Jesus

I took loving Christ Jesus from my Mom and Dad,
They kept Him in their holding sake;
I probably would have gotten close to Him,
But Mom's and Dad's belief was mine to take.

I am surely in love with Him,
As I am close to Him every day;
He is paying attention now to keep me here,
Trying to do everything coming His way.

## *Our Hours Together*

For the importance of your family and life time,
Never avoiding people you see are bright;
For the importance of thought of your hours and mine,
Of each day for us and of each and every night.

The shared hours with you I enjoy that never end,
We discuss stories about our good times that last;
I focus on being a dependable Dad and good friend,
Securing our love of the present and the past.

You take time to enjoy animals and cooking plants,
These are all good and wonderful things we know;
Sun, moon and stars to provide light for us and maybe Santa,
It's like our Love, Christmas Love, that make us go.

So what will you receive at Christmas from me,
Maybe it could be candy, clothes, toys, jewelry, money;
Or it could include hours to share in the future to see,
It will include our Sharing of Love both serious and funny.

## Finding You and Him

I first found Him in my neighborhood,
Walking around with everyone there;
I tried my best to reach Him,
But I was missing the right What, When or Where.

I also found Him in the delivery room,
On my first-born's very first day;
I tried my best to speak to Him,
To get us headed-off in the right way.

I found Him on my many trips,
To nice beaches and to healthy farms;
I tried my best to touch Him,
To get us protection from all the world's harms.

I found Him all across the many miles,
That create gaps and distances between;
I tried my best to see Him,
Along with things I never before have seen.

I found Him while writing my poems,
As I grappled for what to say;
I tried my best to understand Him,
And His wisdom on me to lay.

I found Him at Christmas times,
While spending special moments with you:
If I had not found you and Him,
At Christmas there'd be nothing worthwhile to do.

## *To Serve Him*

Dear Mary I'm writing this letter with love and sincerity,
And I know you must be quite busy now;
I heard your precious Babe was just born last night,
So I need to get an urgent message to you somehow.

I'd like to make you a serious proposition,
And it won't cost you a solitary dime;
Before the Christ Child gets much older,
I'd like to spend with Him a lot of uninterrupted time.

I know what I want might seem to be ridiculous,
But I'll explain myself if you'll give me a chance;
I think I can give Him some important tools for His ministry,
If you'll let me teach Him how to speak English and how to dance.

When He starts His ministry here on earth,
If He can speak English He'll be able to reach many more ears;
You know it's not everyone who can speak Galilean Aromaic,
And to learn it would take most pf us years and years.

From my experience I'd recommend Him learning to Salsa dance,
It would be a tremendous help to Him in many ways;
He could better meet and relate to the millions of Spanish-speaking
    people,
And He could better relax at the end of His hard miracle-working days.

We don't know when His Father will call Him (or us) back home,
So I'm offering to start my services as soon as you choose;
You can be sure that you can trust Him in my loving care,
I'll even provide His English workbook and Salsa shoes.

If you decide to take me up on my offer,
I'll make myself available anytime you want to start;
And if you don't know where to find me,
Just ask Little Jesus, He will always be in my heart.

# 6

*Valentines for Dad's Daughters (21)*

## My Love For You

It encircles me, so completely and unbroken,
It burns forever like a bright glowing flame;
It's a vast sea with no reachable bottom,
It's too special to be given a common name.

It remains forever in my thoughts and my wishes,
I feel its presence in every part of my day;
It feeds and nourishes my whole being,
It influences me in everything and in every way.

I'd surely be nothing without it,
I'd be lost and with nowhere to go;
I'll hold-on to it with all of my being,
It's the surest part of me that I know.

It keeps my glass full and overflowing,
It provides a constant spark in this old heart of mine;
What else can I say so that you understand it?
I Love You, My Sweet Valentine!

## Sound The Trumpet

Sound the trumpet,
Bring ice cream and cake;
Beat on the Drum,
A party we must make.

Roll out the welcome,
Invite everyone in sight;
Tell them to prepare to stay,
We'll party well into the night.

Round up Cupid,
Don't forget his bow;
Prepare plenty of bows,
So he's ready to go.

Sound the trumpet,
A celebration we will do;
I have the World's Best Valentine,
And she is none other than YOU.

# *My Valentine*

We are Valentines,
Valentines true and true;
We've been close forever,
With my heart close to you.

You've been close with your heart,
Close for the greatest love to be;
You're the sweetest in the world,
The most fabulous Valentine for me.

I'm lucky to be in your life,
What more could you ever be;
You're always my Valentine in my life,
The most wonderful love for me.

# Little Heart

When I first saw your tiny little feet,
I thought of your little heart with lots of pride;
When I patted your smooth little bottom,
It was like two little hearts side by side.

When I counted your little baby toes,
I thought of your little heart on the run;
When I saw your sweet little smile,
It reminded me of your little heart having fun.

When I held your tiny little hand,
It was like having your little heart to squeeze;
When I heard your fresh little laugh,
I knew when your heart was being pleased.

When I looked into your bright little eyes,
I imagined your little heart sparkling in the sky;
When I admired your rosy little cheeks,
I saw where your little heart has flowed from your cry.

Now those little things are no longer little,
You've grown up in front of these fatherly eyes of mine;
Your little innocent heart has grown into a big loving one,
More than ever you're My More Special Little Valentine.

## *Mighty Fine*

How much is enough
Of all this crazy old stuff?

How high is the sky
That keeps passing us by?

How wide is the ride
Over to the other side?

How deep is the heep
That the sheep jump over in our sleep?

How hard is the card
That we were dealt in our backyard?

How nice are the mice
When you eat them with spice?

How big is the pig
Who sits high on a twig?

How fine is My Valentine?
Mighty fine, because You are Mine!

## *Nearly Enough?*

Have I told you nearly enough
That I love you with all my heart?
That you're more important than the air I breath?
That from your side I'll never depart?

How I showed you nearly enough
That I'll do anything I need to do?
That I'd give up an arm or eye
To make things right for you?

Have I convinced you nearly enough
That I'll go to any length?
That to keep you safe from all worry and harm
I'll use all my resources and strength?

Have I proven to you nearly enough
That I'd swim the deepest sea?
That I'd climb the highest mountain
To keep you close to me?

Have I said and done nearly enough
To convince you of this love of mine?
That forever and ever I want you to know
That I claim you as My Sweetest Valentine!

## *What Counts?*

We all must keep ourselves going,
And find things in life that are worthwhile;
We all must continue to face the daily grind,
And build up steam to go the next grueling mile.

Reflecting back and looking forward,
Totally-up some of the stuff that really counts;
Memories of many small things and special moments with you
Always provides a lot of special substance that mounts.

A simple question, a smile, a hug, a kiss from you here and there,
At the right time when I was expecting it the least;
A sincere complement, an admiring look and a sincere laugh
Many times have given my heart a bountiful feast.

A daughter like you who loves me as I am
Instead of what I should become and be;
A daughter like you who offers unwavering love
And acts like there is no better Daddy than me.

Some may get their motivation from more money,
From bigger jobs, houses and cars;
But for me just having a Valentine of a daughter like you
Helps keep me going and reaching for the stars.

## Reminders

The sun reminds me
As it rises at the break of day;
The wintry wind reminds me
As it blows cold messages my way.

The green hills remind me
As they stand up to be heard;
The birds remind me
As they chirp an encouraging word.

My drive to work reminds me
As busy life is flowing all around;
The church bell reminds me
As it tolls its welcoming sound.

The tree limbs remind me
As they reach out to comfort me;
The full moon reminds me
As its light shines for all to see.

Our hellos and good-byes remind me
That I love you and you love me;
My heart and soul remind me
That My Valentine you will always be.

# Sweet Angel

Some say you're not any Angel,
And I wonder what they mean;
Is it something they think they've seen in you,
Or something they've never seen?

Have they never seen your halo
Glowing with compassion and love?
Have they never felt your comforting wings
Lifting their spirits to heights above?

Have they missed having a kiss of yours
When it's time for good-bye or good night?
How they never saw you react to a poem
Describing a tender moment or sight?

Do they see you through different eyes
Than the ones here in my silly old head?
Do they not know your true loving heart
And judge you by some other heart instead?

Do they not think of you as a Sweet Angel
Like I do when I think of the daughter of mine?
Well if I'm wrong and you're just a Sweet Angel,
I still want you as My Special Valentine!

# *Ubiquitous*

It's with me in the morning,
When I first roll out of bed;
It's with me when I shower,
And when I shave my ugly head.

It's with me when I'm at work,
Bringing home our monthly pay;
It's with me during my work-outs
In my bedroom gym each day.

It's with me when I'm on the golf course,
In the lawn mowing, and at night when I pray;
It's with me watching ball games,
It's obviously here with me to stay.

It's with me in my heart,
In my head and in this soul of mine;
You are always with me my special Sweetie,
You"re My Sweet Ubiquitous Valentine.

# *You Are My Valentine*

In my younger years I knew some about love,
But I had never known much about Valentine;
So I had never had a relationship with Cupid,
And the real sense of love had never been mine.

But things were a little different in my older years,
Things really changed when you were born;
When our first Valentine Day came along,
My life looked different and my previous feelings worn.

Today is no different and is addressed by my dreams,
Today Cupid follows you continually for you and me;
And I pay close attention about where you are,
Sharing our love as Valentines we will always be.

## Valentine Swaps

I'll give you a penny for your thoughts
If you'll be honest and true;
I'll swap you a nickel for a kiss,
And a nickel more for each kiss from you.

I'll trade you a dime for your time,
If you'll focus your attention on me;
I'll toss you a quarter for a hug,
If you'll let it be as close as can be.

I'll hand you a dollar for your love,
If you'll promise that you'll accept mine;
I'll give you every last bit of my heart,
If you'll just be My Valentine.

## *All of My Family Valentines*

I think of You often,
As I fly around in the skies;
I never find anyone else as beautiful,
As I find You filling up my heart and eyes.

I stay as close to You as I can,
I keep You here as each day will start;
I keep You in my favorable being to stay,
Hoping to get myself forever in Your heart.

No one can overcome Your special being,
Your beauty is above every other Valentine;
I don't know what I'd do without You,
In keeping Your heart and love close to mine.

# Valentine Would Ya's

Would Ya ever, ever call me,
If I never left messages on your phone?
Would Ya come looking for me,
If I was lost and all alone?

Would Ya stay close by my side,
If I was sick, scared, or worse yet?
Would Ya stick with me,
If I lost all of my money on a bet?

Would Ya bother to defend me,
If bad things of me were said?
Would Ya dare to tell me how you really feel,
Or would Ya tell me a little lie instead?

Would Ya really forgive me,
If I made a huge mistake?
Would Ya try to understand,
Or suggest that a walk I should take?

Would Ya cut out your own heart,
If it would save this life of mine?
I already know that you certainly would,
And so would I, My Most Special Valentine.

## When (Our Promises To You)

When my Valentine comes,
Will I have every chance,
To skip, hop and prance
And with my Valentine dance?

When my Valentine calls
With a message just for me,
With a gift to give lovingly,
Will I be free to agree?

When my Valentine looks,
Will I have a fitting gown,
Jewels enough to make a crown,
And a smile that will knock him down?

When my Valentine asks
To take me by the hand,
Will I get to say YES and
Go walking barefoot in the sand?

When my Valentine leaves
Taking with him his precious heart,
While leaving in mine a nasty dart,
Will I be allowed another start?

When a new Valentine comes,
Will Mom and Dad still be my friends,
Solving problems and making amends,
Sticking by me to the very end?

# Valentine If'uns

If'un I was a bee,
I'd give you lots of honey;
If'un I was a bank,
I'd fill your purse with money.

If'un I was a bird,
I'd teach you how to fly;
If'un I was a baker,
I'd bake you a raspberry pie.

If'un I was a dog,
I'd chase you all night and day;
If'un I I was smart enough,
I'd show you the right way.

If'un I was a young woman,
I'd want your beauty to be mine;
If'un I was a young man,
I'd want to be your Valentine.

## *All Valentine For Me*

It's always time to love with you,
It's that way for us to be one;
I always feel that we are Valentines,
Great lovers for us never to be gone.

You are great to be inside me,
I always see the best of you;
Who else could be more of a Valentine,
Than you as a lover best for me to do.

Being able to be a lover with you,
It's also so great for me to see;
Loving you is all Valentine for me,
Nothing more lovers for us to be.

# *Always My Valentine*

It's always time to love with you,
It's that way for us to be one;
I always feel that we are Valentines,
Great lovers for us never to be gone.

You are great to be inside me,
I always see the best of you;
Who else could be more of a Valentine,
Than you as a lover best for me to do.

Being able to be a lover with you,
It's also so great for me to see;
Loving you is all Valentine for me,
Nothing more lovers for us to be.

# Would You Rather?

Would you rather be My Sweet Valentine
Or a bump on an old rotten log?
Would you rather be My Sweet Valentine
Or the curl on the tail of a hog?

Would you rather be My Sweet Valentine
Or a tick on a possum's thick skin?
Would you rather be My Sweet Valentine
Or a hole that a snake crawls in?

Would you rather be My Sweet Valentine
Or a mole on a fat lady's nose?
Would you rather be My Sweet Valentine
Or a wart between a football player's toes?

Would you rather be My Sweet Valentine
Or the hair on a donkey's behind?
Would you rather be My Sweet Valentine
Or a big sewer rat who's just gone blind?

Would you rather be My Sweet Valentine
Or a pan full of Mommy's stir-fry?
Would you rather be My Sweet Valentine
Or lizard skin hung out to dry?

Just admit your Dad is "Ex-traod-in-are"
Just say you would rather be mine;
I know you know nothing else can "Compare"
With being old Dad's Sweet Valentine!

## *Birdie Do*

Birdie do me a favor,
Birdie do, please, Birdie do;
Sing me a cheerful Birdie song,
And I'll give a smile to you.

Sit awhile upon my shoulder,
And I'll give you a wink or two;
Rub softly against my red rosy cheeks,
And I'll fly through the sky with you.

Tickle me pink with your feathery wings,
And I'll laugh until I turn blue;
Birdie do, be my sweet little Valentine,
And I'll always take care of you.

# The Reason Why

Valentine, Valentine,
You should be here with me;
When you're far away,
My heart is as blue as the sea.

Valentine, Valentine,
You are always on my mind:
When I let my thoughts wonder,
Memories of you are the best ones I find.

Valentine, Valentine,
My heart would be totally useless without you:
It would be just a dark, cold chamber,
With nothing to love, nothing meaningful to do.

Valentine, Valentine,
You always have so much comfort and joy to give:
Valentine, Valentine,
You are the reason I exist and why I want to live.

# 7

*Easter for Dad's Daughters (7)*

## Ten Thousand in One

If I had a star out of heaven,
And a cup of raspberries and cream;
If I had a Bouquet of Easter wishes,
And a fairytale in my dream.

If I had a perfect little daisy,
And a rainbow on a long string;
If I had a vase of fresh roses,
And my very own Robin for Spring.

If I had a cupcake with soft pink icing,
And a shiny pancake with a fancy red bow;
If I had a mellon juicy and ripe,
And a secret place far away to go.

If I had a soft cloud and a moon beam,
And a parade and a party for fun;
I'd trade it all for a kiss from my Daughter,
You're ten thousand treasures wrapped in One!

# Easter Things to Me

The bunny brought my basket,
Full of candy and colored eggs;
The tailor made my brand new suit,
To hide my fat tummy and boney legs.

The choir sang my favorite hymn,
That my Granddaddy used to sing;
My Reverend preached a sermon,
About the forgiveness that Easters bring.

Grandma cooked my favorite meal,
The best I did ever see;
So I sent the Easter Bunny back,
To bring my special daughter to me.

## *Miracles For Me*

It's a miracle that Jesus was ever born,
Are that He died for you and me;
It's a miracle that Jesus rose up again,
And that His love is still here for us to see.

It's a miracle that you are my daughter,
And that you want me to write, visit and call;
It's a miracle that you still call me Daddy,
And that you still care and love me at all.

It's these miracles at Spring that I cherish,
Easter flowers and the days of one Birth;
It's these miracles for which I am most thankful,
Without them and you my life would have little worth.

# The Perfect Easter

Baskets and colored eggs,
Fancy bonnets, dresses and bows;
Lipstick, powder and perfume,
Bright polish on fingers and toes.

Little chicks and ducklings,
Little bunnies made of fluff;
Beans made of jelly,
And lots of chocolate stuff.

Green grass and flowers,
Robins and honey bees;
Warm wind and sunshine,
Pretty blooms on the trees.

Hiding and hunting,
Finding surprises, too;
A perfect Easter for me
Is a basket full of you.

## *Easter Bunny Is Coming*

The bright sun is shining,
The green grass is growing;
The Spring rain is falling,
The warm wind is blowing.

Daddy Rabbit is hopping,
Mother Hen is laying;
Butterflies are dancing,
Dogs and cats are playing.

Fresh flowers are watching,
Colored eggs are waiting;
Baby ducks are hopping,
Little girls are anticipating.

Red robins are chirping,
Honey bees are humming;
Mom and Dad are singing,
Easter Bunny is coming.

## Cottontail Easter

You could have been an Easter egg,
Colored purple, orange, yellow, and blue;
You could have been a little basket,
With pine grass and a toy chick or two.

You could have been a pretty bonnet,
Made with straw and a long navy bow;
You could have been a candy rabbit
Of milk chocolate and soft marshmallow.

You could have been an Easter flower,
A white lily or a bright daffodil;
You could have been a little jelly bean,
Or a cute dress with a satine frail.

You could have been a cottontail.
With not a single little word to say;
You could have been most anything,
And I would still like you anyway;

## Happy Duckies

Early Spring mornings are mighty fond,
For all the duckies down on the pond.

The water has thawed of its winter ice,
It's just wet and wild enough to be ducky nice.

The minnows are hatching as are the frogs,
Offering good hunting near the bank and around the logs.

For insects and worms provide a special treat,
Lots of delightful goodies to snatch up and eat.

No grades to make or cheerleading tryouts to pass,
No troubles and worries to create that stinky Duck's gas.

Life's got to be simpler for a Ducky Daughter and Dad,
I'd guess that being a ducky mustn't be so bad.

Easter surely makes duckies happy too,
Christ Jesus has risen for duckies and for me and you.

# 8

## Thanksgiving for Dad's Daughters (5)

## Can't Forget You

Can't forget the party hats
On the eve of each new year;
Can't forget the sweethearts,
When Valentine's Day is near.

Can't forget the colored eggs,
On Easter Sunday morn;
Can't forget the candles,
On the day that you were born.

Can't forget to fly the flag,
On every Fourth of July;
And when it's Halloween night
Trick-or-Treat we can't deny.

Can't forget the Manager Child,
On Christmas and on Sundays, too;
And can't forget during Thanksgiving
How Lucky I am to have You.

## *Gather Up Sweet Thanksgiving*

Gather up the fallen leaves
That pile-up in our yard;
Gather up the silly poems
That fill-up all our cards.

Gather up the sunshine
To brighten our Winter blues;
Gather up our phone calls,
That bring me your weekly news.

Gather up the morning frost
That comes with Fall-time weather;
Gather up our special visits
That keep us close together.

Gather up the turkeys,
The eggs, rolls, and corn;
Gather up the drawings
So they don't get lost or torn.

Gather up the pumpkins
That go into Grandma's pie;
Gather up my sweet Daughter
Before Thanksgiving passes by.

# Happy Daddy Pilgrim

The night before I was born,
An Angel came to let me decide;
To be a Pilgrim in a Pilgrim's hat
Or an Indian wearing a Buffalo hide.

At first the choice seemed so simple,
An Indian was what I wanted to be;
Running wild, screaming loud and riding ponies
Seemed like lots of great fun to me.

The Pilgrim's life seemed such a bore,
Always working and tending the fort;
You know growing corn, catching turkeys,
Picking berries, raising pumpkins, and things of that sort.

But I discussed my choices with the Angel that night,
She reminded me of a thought to help convince;
"An Indian has features and a Pilgrim has daughters,"
Sp I've been a happy Daddy Pilgrim ever since.

## Blessings

What else could I ever hope for
That I haven't already got;
What else could I ever ask for,
So much Is mine, so little Is Not.

My cup is overflowing
With many friends, things and stuff;
Still there are times I feel
That all I have is not enough.

But every time I return my thanks
For what I am, have and do;
I'm reminded of how Blessed I am at Thanksgiving
Just to have a Daughter like you.

## *You're a Real Gas*

You always provide us a Laugh,
You always wear a Big Thanksgiving Smile;
You're always willing to help out with the Work,
Even if it's going to take a Long While.

You're always ready to Go,
And always willing to Play;
Whenever and wherever you're Around,
You make it a Much Better Day.

You make us feel Important,
You treat us like we're First Class;
We're so thankful you're our Daughter,
You're a great girl and always a Real Gas.

# 9

## The Ending of Dad's Poems

## *The Greatness of Dad's Girls*

Dad's girls are close by for 18 years or more,
They are there with you daily for a family score.

They are full of happiness, beauty, love, and fun,
Ready to go for it with tossing, flying and run.

They have dreams and goals to meet the best,
Working real hard and doing everything for rest.

So what do you need to do to keep things swell,
It's up to you to make it all to turnout well.

So always keep your part serious by Christ Jesus' call,
Your heart and hers will always find lots of love in it all.

www.ingramcontent.com/pod-product-compliance
Lightning Source LLC
Chambersburg PA
CBHW021113080526
44587CB00010B/503